D0860380

A Guide to
AMERICAN STATES

Idaho

THE GEM STATE

MEDIA ENHANCED BOOKS
AV2 BY WEIGL
ADDED VALUE · AUDIO VISUAL

www.av2books.com

AV² provides enriched content that supplements and complements this book. Weigl's AV² books strive to create inspired learning and engage young minds in a total learning experience.

Your AV² Media Enhanced books come alive with...

Audio
Listen to sections of the book read aloud.

Key Words
Study vocabulary, and complete a matching word activity.

Video
Watch informative video clips.

Quizzes
Test your knowledge.

Go to **www.av2books.com,** and enter this book's unique code.

Embedded Weblinks
Gain additional information for research.

Slide Show
View images and captions, and prepare a presentation.

BOOK CODE

G159081

Try This!
Complete activities and hands-on experiments.

... and much, much more!

AV² by Weigl brings you media enhanced books that support active learning.

Published by AV² by Weigl
350 5th Avenue, 59th Floor
New York, NY 10118
Website: www.av2books.com   www.weigl.com

Library of Congress Cataloging-in-Publication Data

Foran, Jill.
  Idaho / Jill Foran.
     p. cm. -- (A guide to American states)
  Includes index.
  ISBN 978-1-61690-784-6 (hardcover) -- ISBN 978-1-61690-460-9 (online)
  1. Idaho--Juvenile literature. I. Title.
  F746.3.F675 2011
  979.6--dc23
                              2011018325

Printed in the United States of America in North Mankato, Minnesota

052011
WEP180511

Project Coordinator Jordan McGill
Art Director Terry Paulhus

Photo Credits
Every reasonable effort has been made to trace ownership and to obtain permission to reprint copyright material. The publishers would be pleased to have any errors or omissions brought to their attention so that they may be corrected in subsequent printings.

Weigl acknowledges Getty Images as its primary image supplier for this title.

Contents

AV² Book Code 2

Introduction 4

Where Is Idaho? 6

Mapping Idaho 8

The Land 10

Climate 12

Natural Resources 14

Plants 16

Animals 18

Tourism 20

Industry 22

Goods and Services 24

American Indians 26

Explorers and Missionaries 28

Early Settlers 30

Notable People 32

Population 34

Politics and Government 36

Cultural Groups 38

Arts and Entertainment 40

Sports 42

National Averages Comparison 44

How to Improve My Community 45

Exercise Your Mind! 46

Words to Know / Index 47

Log on to www.av2books.com 48

Idaho has 80 recognized mountain ranges, with a mean elevation of about 5,000 feet above sea level.

Introduction

I daho is known for its natural beauty. It is a mountainous state, filled with breathtaking peaks and magnificent forests and waterways, including the Snake, Salmon, Clearwater, Payette, and Boise rivers. Flower-filled meadows and other areas of open wilderness add even more variety to the landscape. More than a thousand miles of state roads are designated as "scenic byways."

The product that Idaho is most famous for is probably potatoes. Vast potato fields spread across the southeastern region. Idaho potatoes account for almost one-third of the national potato production and are found on dinner tables all over the world.

The Snake River outlines a small section of the Idaho-Washington border and about half of the Idaho-Oregon boundary.

Redfish Lake is one of many glacial lakes in the state. When the glaciers retreated, they left ice in hollows between hills. The ice melted and formed lakes.

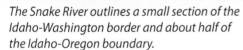

Nicknames for Idaho include the Potato State and the Spud State. However, the state's economy does not rely on spuds. Idaho's official nickname is the Gem State. Many **precious** and semiprecious stones are found in Idaho's mountains, valleys, and plains. Mining valuable gemstones, minerals, and metals, such as silver and lead, is a big business in the state. Manufacturing is also important. Idaho's products include computers and electronics.

One of the largest diamonds ever found in the United States was discovered near McCall. It weighed nearly 20 carats. However, gemstones are not the only things that shine in Idaho. The sparkling lakes, gleaming waterfalls, stunning landscapes, booming service industries, and lively people help to make Idaho a true gem of a state.

Where Is Idaho?

Idaho is located in the northwestern United States. Its name may have origins in American Indian culture, though historians cannot agree on this. Some say the name resembles a Shoshone phrase of welcome. Others say the politician George M. Willing invented the word. In the early 1860s, Willing supposedly told the U.S. Congress that Idaho was an American Indian word meaning "gem of the mountains." Willing had an interest in mining and hoped to call the Colorado region Idaho. Though Congress rejected the name, it caught on in the north, and the mines at the Clearwater and Salmon rivers, in what is now central Idaho, became known as the Idaho Mines. Eventually, the name came into use for the entire area.

The Snake River played an important role in the nation's westward expansion. Pioneers followed the river to the Pacific Northwest.

In 1863 the vast region including what is now Idaho, Montana, and Wyoming was called the Idaho Territory. In 1868 both Montana and Wyoming became their own territories, giving Idaho its present borders.

In 1864 both the Northern Pacific and the Union Pacific railroads laid track in the area. This made it easier for new settlers to travel to the region. The railroads also began to ship out Idaho's minerals, lumber, and farm products. After the railways were completed, large communities sprang up. In 1890 Idaho became a state. By that time its population had risen to about 90,000 people.

Now, all major cities in the state have commercial airports. The busiest airport in Idaho is the Boise Air Terminal. **Transcontinental** railroads serve the state. Ships from the Pacific Ocean reach Idaho at the port of Lewiston, on the border with Washington, by traveling up the Columbia and Snake rivers.

Idaho is the 11th largest state in land area.

The land area of Idaho is 82,747 square miles.

The highest peak is Borah Peak. It is 12,662 feet above sea level.

The star garnet, the state gem, is found in northern Idaho. The only other place where the star garnet is found in large quantities is the country of India.

The Idaho Territory was split into the Idaho, Montana, and Wyoming territories because the region was too large to effectively govern with one governmental body.

Many of the tracks built to service the mining and lumber industries in the early 1900s are no longer used. Some of the older tracks are being reopened for leisure and tourism travel.

Mapping Idaho

A number of major highways run through Idaho. Interstate 15 and U.S. 91, U.S. 93, and U.S. 95 run from north to south. Interstates 84, 86, and 90 and U.S. 12, U.S. 20, U.S. 26, and U.S. 30 run east-west. Idaho shares its borders with seven neighbors. Montana and Wyoming form Idaho's eastern boundary, while Oregon and Washington form its western boundary. Utah and Nevada lie to the south, and Canada lies to the north.

Sites and Symbols

STATE SEAL
Idaho

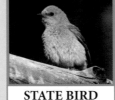

STATE BIRD
Mountain Bluebird

STATE FLOWER
Syringa

STATE FLAG
Idaho

STATE HORSE
Appaloosa

STATE TREE
Western White Pine

Nickname The Gem State

Motto *Esto Perpetua* (It Is Perpetuated)

Song "Here We Have Idaho," words by Albert J. Tompkins and McKinley Helm and music by Sallie Hume Douglas

Entered the Union July 3, 1890, as the 43rd state

Capital Boise

Population (2010 Census) 1,567,582 Ranked 39th state

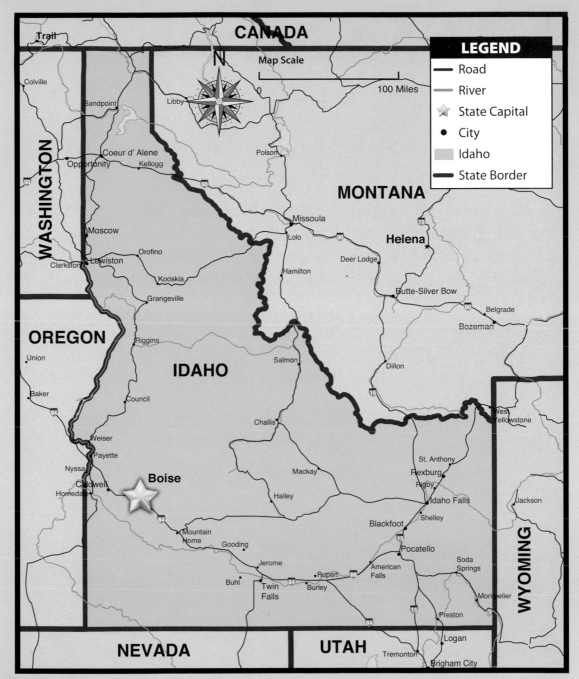

CANADA

Trail

Colville

Sandpoint

Libby

N

Map Scale

100 Miles

LEGEND
Road
River
State Capital
City
Idaho
State Border

WASHINGTON

Coeur d' Alene
Opportunity
Kellogg

90

90

Polson

Missoula

MONTANA

Lolo

Helena

Moscow

Orofino

Deer Lodge

90

Clarkston Lewiston

Kooskia

Hamilton

Grangeville

Butte-Silver Bow

Belgrade

Bozeman

OREGON

Riggins

IDAHO

Salmon

Dillon

Union

Baker

Council

Challis

84

West Yellowstone

15

Weiser

Payette

Nyssa

Caldwell

Homedale

Boise

Mackay

Hailey

St. Anthony
Rexburg
Rigby
Idaho Falls
Shelley

Jackson

Mountain Home

Gooding

84

Jerome

Buhl

Twin Falls

Burley

84

Rupert

American Falls

86

Blackfoot

15

Pocatello

Soda Springs

Montpelier

WYOMING

Preston

15

84

Logan

NEVADA

UTAH

Tremonton

Brigham City

STATE CAPITAL

When the **capitol** in Boise was constructed, starting in 1905, builders used sandstone from local quarries. On the central part of the building, the sandstone was shaped above the base to look like the logs stacked in the log cabins of the early settlers.

United States

Idaho

Hawai'i   Alaska

The Land

Idaho's landscape is both beautiful and varied. Towering mountains, vast sand dunes, deep river canyons, underground ice caves, and prehistoric lava beds contribute to the state's diverse beauty.

The densely forested Rocky Mountains cover much of Idaho. In contrast to the mountains is the Snake River Plain. This plain sweeps across southern Idaho in an arc that covers the width of the state. It is a broad, treeless expanse of land that includes some of the most desolate areas of the northwestern United States.

PALOUSE REGION

The Palouse region is a hilly area in northern Idaho. It is covered with farms.

IDAHO PANHANDLE NATIONAL FOREST

Idaho Panhandle National Forest is one of 13 national forests within the state. An additional national forest is partly in Idaho but also in Montana.

HEAVEN'S GATE

At Heaven's Gate, on the Lewis and Clark Trail, visitors can see the four states of Idaho, Montana, Oregon, and Washington.

SAWTOOTH RANGE

The Sawtooth Range is part of the Sawtooth National Recreation Area.

Idaho's whitewater rivers cover 3,100 miles. Idaho boasts more miles of white water than any other of the 48 contiguous states.

North America's deepest river gorge is in Idaho. Hells Canyon is situated along the Snake River on the Idaho-Oregon border. It reaches a maximum depth of 7,900 feet.

The Idaho mountains force air to rise up to cooler altitudes. Cool air does not hold moisture well, so rain or snow falls. This water ends up in streams and lakes.

Climate

I daho's climate is mild. Winds from the Pacific Ocean bring warm sea air to the state, and the high mountains along the eastern border block out cold winter air coming from the north and the east. Summers are generally warm, with the highest temperatures occurring in the plains and valleys. The mountains are usually cooler and wetter throughout the year. In winter the mountains can receive enormous amounts of snow.

Even mild states have their extremes, however. As of 2010, the hottest temperature ever recorded in Idaho was at Orofino on July 28, 1934. It was 118° Fahrenheit. The coldest recorded temperature was −60° F at Island Park Dam on January 18, 1943.

Average Annual Temperatures Across Idaho

In Idaho, the average annual temperature is generally in the mid-40s, measured in degrees Fahrenheit. But some spots are cooler. Stanley is about 130 miles east of Boise, in the Sawtooth Range. Why might it make sense that Stanley is somewhat cooler?

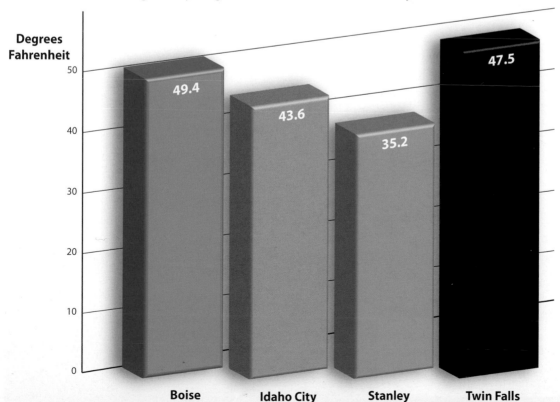

Degrees Fahrenheit

- Boise: 49.4
- Idaho City: 43.6
- Stanley: 35.2
- Twin Falls: 47.5

Natural Resources

Natural resources have long been the basis for Idaho's economy. Water is the most important of these resources. More than 2,000 lakes combine with the large rivers and their tributaries to supply the state with plenty of water for **hydroelectric power**, **irrigation**, and recreation.

The Snake River is approximately 1,040 miles long. In addition to Idaho, it runs through Wyoming, Oregon, Washington, and small parts of Nevada and Utah.

Water plays an essential role in Idaho's agricultural production. The most fertile soil in the state is found in sections of the Snake River Plain. Because the plain is very dry, an irrigation system has been constructed to bring water to the area.

With irrigation, the soils in the Snake River Plain produce crops of wheat, fruit, potatoes, and other vegetables. Soils in other parts of the state are not as well suited for farming. The soils in the mountain regions, for example, are thin and unable to sustain crops.

Idaho's mountains offer other natural resources however. The forests provide timber, and the land is filled with minerals. Valuable mineral deposits can be found in all of Idaho's counties. Silver, gold, lead, and phosphate are among the most important mineral resources in the state.

Wheat is a major crop in Idaho. In 2010 the state produced more than 100 million bushels of wheat.

Plants

People in Idaho enjoy some of the largest unspoiled natural areas in the United States. Forestland covers more than two-fifths of the state. These forests are mostly in the mountains and contain such evergreens as Douglas firs, pines, spruces, and western larches. Idaho's valleys contain birches, willows, and aspens. Some of the state's red cedar trees are hundreds of years old.

The dry climate of southern Idaho supports sagebrush on the plains. Sagebrush is a shrubby plant that is able to grow in places that receive little rainfall. Larger plants and trees can be found along the rivers. Native plants in Idaho include the wildflowers sticky geranium, rosy pussytoes, blue columbine, and prairie smoke. Idaho fescue, bottlebrush squirreltail, and little bluestem are among the grasses that grow in the state.

BUTTERCUPS

Buttercups are common wildflowers in the moist regions of Idaho.

WESTERN RED CEDARS

Western red cedars grow very slowly and live for hundreds of years.

QUAKING ASPEN

Quaking aspen are so-named because the flat stems of their leaves cause the leaves to tremble even in a light breeze.

DWARF BUCKWHEAT

Dwarf buckwheat grows in the lava rock at Craters of the Moon National Monument.

The Idaho Forest Service encourages people to draw, paint, or photograph native plants rather than pick them.

In the fall, groves of aspen trees change color at the same time. This is because each tree in a grove is a clone of a "founding" tree.

Idaho sagebrush is being studied for its ability to fight fungal infections in plants and people.

The Western white pine is the state tree of Idaho. It is found in abundance north of the Clearwater River.

Along the lava trails of the Snake River Plain, certain areas lack soil, yet a variety of plants and flowers still grow. Hardy wildflowers grow in the cracks, along with ferns, mosses, lichens, and various grasses.

Native plants have been cultivated along Idaho's roadways to decrease soil erosion. Most of the plants selected are flowering plants, such as Indian blanketflower.

Animals

Idaho's natural areas are home to many kinds of animals. It is one of the few places in the United States where many large mammals roam freely. Moose, grizzly and black bears, elks, cougars, and reindeer live in Idaho's forests. Smaller animals of the forest include beavers, minks, otters, muskrats, and raccoons. Mule deer and white-tailed deer can be found throughout the state.

Idaho is careful to preserve its nature and wildlife. The Snake River Birds of Prey Natural Conservation Area is home to the world's largest concentration of nesting raptors. Eagles, ospreys, hawks, and falcons soar through this protected area. Other wildlife preserves in the state include the Grays Lake National Wildlife Refuge and the Kootenai Wildlife Refuge.

CUTHROAT TROUT

The cutthroat trout is the state fish of Idaho. It was named for the colorful slash on the underside of its jaw.

MONARCH BUTTERFLY

The monarch butterfly was named the state insect in 1992. A monarch can migrate many miles in its short lifetime.

CONDOR

Condors were once common in the American Far West but are now quite rare. To increase their numbers, condors are being bred at the World Center for Birds of Prey, in Boise, for release into the wild.

GRIZZLY BEAR

Grizzly bears can still be found in Idaho in the northern mountains and in the east, near Yellowstone National Park, but the bears have become rare.

Idaho's state horse is the Appaloosa. The Nez Percé people, who are native to Idaho, are renowned breeders of the spotted horse known as the Appaloosa.

Otters can be found in a number of Idaho's rivers. They feed on a variety of animals, from small mammals to frogs and birds.

American white pelicans nest in colonies on islands in Blackfoot Reservoir, Lake Walcott, and other sites in southern Idaho.

Tourism

Visitors come to Idaho to see its many natural wonders, breathe its fresh air, and explore the mountains. Both tourists and residents take part in outdoor recreation in the state.

Idaho's caves are popular attractions. Some of the state's caves were formed by flowing lava from volcanoes that erupted long ago. Inside, these caves can be surprisingly cool, even on a hot day.

One of Idaho's most popular natural wonders is Craters of the Moon National Monument and Preserve. This area, in the eastern half of the Snake River Plain, is one of the most unusual geological formations in the United States. Volcanic eruptions and lava flows began at this site about 15,000 years ago and continued until about 2,000 years ago. Today visitors can explore the landscape left behind by these eruptions.

CRATERS OF THE MOON

Craters of the Moon National Monument sits on the largest lava field in the continental United States.

SUN VALLEY RESORT

Nestled in Bald and Dollar mountains, the Sun Valley Resort is a popular destination for winter skiers.

HORSEBACK RIDING TRAILS

Outfitters offer a variety of horseback-riding experiences, from trails through scenic Idaho mountains to cattle roundups.

IDAHO'S GHOST TOWNS

In Idaho's ghost towns, visitors can walk along empty streets and inspect the old, rustic buildings where miners and their families once gathered.

The Old Idaho Penitentiary, in Boise, is open to visitors. The jail functioned for 103 years and housed some of the state's worst criminals. It closed its doors in 1973.

Balanced Rock is a natural **phenomenon** that attracts tourists. Over time the bottom section of the massive rock has been worn away, giving the impression that it might fall over at any minute.

U.S. Highway 12 follows much the same path that explorers Meriwether Lewis and William Clark took through the state's Bitterroot Mountains on their famous expedition of 1804–1806.

At Minnetonka Cave, visitors can walk through beautiful limestone rooms that have been created by underground rivers.

At the old Sierra Silver Mine in Wallace, tourists can explore an underground mine and experience what it was like to be a miner more than a century ago.

Industry

Agriculture has long been important in Idaho's economy. Potatoes are the leading crop, and Idaho generally leads the nation in potato production. Idaho farmers also harvest great quantities of barley, sugar beets, and wheat. In addition, Idaho ranks among the top states in sales of dairy products. Food processing has become one of the leading manufacturing activities in the state. This includes the processing of potato products.

Industries in Idaho
Value of Goods and Services in Millions of Dollars

Growing food is essential, but industries in which workers provide services to other people have become larger contributors to Idaho's economy in recent years. Why do you think the service industries have become so important in the state?

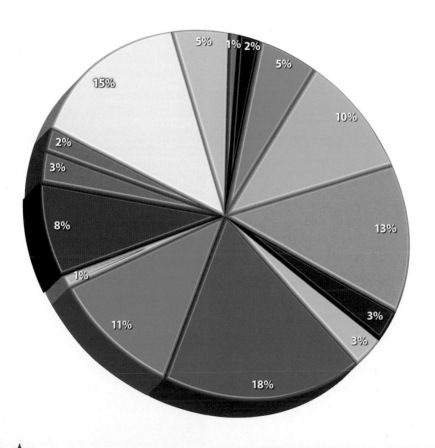

LEGEND

Agriculture, Forestry, and Fishing $2,451

Mining $752

Utilities $873

Construction $2,734

Manufacturing $5,641

Wholesale and Retail Trade $7,187

Transportation $1,585

Media and Entertainment $1,632

Finance, Insurance, and Real Estate $9,806

Professional and Technical Services $6,201

Education $355

Health Care $4,082

Hotels and Restaurants $1,449

Other Services $1,291

Government $7,967

TOTAL $54,006

People all over North America enjoy french fries processed in Idaho. Other food-processing plants in the state include sugar-beet refineries, meat and poultry processors, dairies, and canning and freezing companies. Most of these plants are in the southern part of the state, near the agricultural areas.

Manufacturing, including lumber products and chemicals, is quite important to the state's economy. The Boise area is active in the manufacturing of high-technology products, such as computers and computer software. The entire state is active with service industries, such as health care and tourism.

A sawmill on the Clearwater River provides raw materials for businesses such as Clearwater Paper, a Lewiston company that makes tissue products.

I DIDN'T KNOW THAT!

The Silver Valley, in northern Idaho, historically has been one of the top-ten mining districts in the world. Precious metals have been mined in the area since the late 1800s.

The average American eats more than 100 pounds of potatoes per year. The potato, Idaho's most important crop, is used in a wide variety of foods.

The majority of Idaho's potatoes are processed into frozen or dried potato products, which are then exported to other countries and states.

The Idaho Department of Labor has identified the hot jobs for the coming years as positions in health care.

Tourism employs more than 260,000 Idahoans, according to the Idaho Department of Commerce. The great outdoors is Idaho's greatest draw.

Goods and Services

Idaho produces a great variety of wood products, including plywood, poles, boxes, furniture, and railroad ties. Wood pulp and paper are also produced in the state. The majority of the state's lumber mills are located in the panhandle, which is the tall and narrow northern part of the state.

The bulk of Idaho's products that are shipped out of the state, such as farm products, minerals, and lumber, travel by train and truck. Other products are shipped by **barge**. Lewiston, in the north, is the major port town. In fact, it is known as the Seaport of Idaho even though it is almost 500 miles from the Pacific Ocean. Today large ships still carry grain and lumber out of Lewiston.

Hells Canyon Dam and others control water flow and create hydroelectricity. Idaho has 17 hydroelectric power plants.

Boise is a manufacturing center for high technology goods, such as computers, because it is a university town. Educated labor is readily available.

In 1915 engineers built a canal on the Columbia River and a series of dams and **locks** on both the Columbia and Snake rivers. These allowed barges and tugboats to transport farm and forest products out of Lewiston to the Pacific Ocean. Today large ships still carry grain and lumber out of Lewiston.

Idaho has a number of private and public colleges and three major universities. The large universities are Boise State University, Idaho State University, and the University of Idaho. Some of the educational programs in Idaho are connected to the state's leading business activities. For example, students at the University of Idaho can earn degrees in mining or forestry.

I DIDN'T KNOW THAT!

The research of students and professors in Idaho's universities has improved the state's farming output. Researchers have developed new and improved varieties of wheat, barley, oats, and other important crops.

Boise Cascade, which has its headquarter in Boise, is a major manufacturer of wood products and many types of building materials.

Hydroelectricity is Idaho's chief source of power.

The world's first nuclear power plant went into operation in 1951 near Arco. This town became the first community in the world to have its electricity generated by atomic energy.

The state seal was changed in 1957 to show that mining, agriculture, and forestry were the main industries. Today, service industries are also a major part of the economy.

Micron, a manufacturer of semiconductors for computers, is based in Boise but has a global reach. Their core business is memory technology for mobile, computer, and industrial products.

American Indians

American Idaho's earliest inhabitants roamed the land thousands of years ago. While digging in southern Idaho's Wilson Butte Cave, **archaeologists** discovered pieces of pottery, jagged arrowheads, and other tools. Some of these items were more than 13,000 years old.

Other areas of the state also contain compelling proof of early cultures. Ancient rock carvings called **petroglyphs** and rock drawings called **pictographs** can be found along the Salmon and Snake rivers. Ancient art has been found in other regions of the state, too.

Early Hells Canyon inhabitants left paintings in caves. The artwork was a way to tell hunting stories.

Several American Indian groups lived in the Idaho region at the time European explorers arrived. The Nez Percé occupied the central region, while the Shoshone, Bannock, and Paiute lived in the south. The Coeur d'Alene, Pend d'Oreille, and Kootenai lived in the north. These groups relied on Idaho's natural resources. They hunted wildlife in the forests and prairies and fished in the lakes and rivers.

American Indians in what is now Idaho likely saw their first horses, brought by Spanish explorers, in the 1700s. The use of horses forever changed their lives and cultures. Horses gave American Indians greater mobility while hunting and made it easier to trade with groups from other parts of the Northwest.

Appaloosa horses were prized by the Nez Percé, a fact noted by American explorers Meriwether Lewis and William Clark.

The largest of Idaho's American Indian groups were the Nez Percé and the Shoshone.

Cradleboards, made of buckskin and willow branches, were used by the Shoshone to keep their babies warm and secure while traveling.

The name Nez Percé means "Pierced Nose" in French. French explorers mistakenly gave this name to the Nez Percé after encountering another tribe. In fact, the Nez Percé did not usually pierce their noses to wear jewelry.

At first the American Indians were friendly toward new settlers. As time went on, however, many problems arose.

City of Rocks was part of the Oregon Trail, which led settlers from the East through Idaho.

Explorers and Missionaries

The American explorers Meriwether Lewis and William Clark were the first people of European descent to explore the Idaho region. In 1804 U.S. President Thomas Jefferson sent Lewis and Clark on an **expedition** to explore part of the Louisiana Territory, which the United States had just bought from France, and to try to find a water route to the Pacific Ocean. Starting near St. Louis, the explorers sailed up the Missouri River and then moved westward over rough terrain. They traveled through Idaho's challenging Bitterroot Mountains. This leg of their journey was especially difficult and they endured many hardships along the way, including drastic food shortages and deep snow. They eventually reached the Pacific Ocean before returning to St. Louis in 1806.

In the early 1800s missionaries from the eastern United States became interested in the Idaho region. In 1836, Henry Harmon Spalding, a Presbyterian minister, arrived in the area with his wife, Eliza. The Spaldings established the first mission in Idaho, Lapwai Mission, near the site of present-day Lewiston.

Timeline of Settlement

Exploration

1804 President Thomas Jefferson sends Lewis and Clark on an expedition to explore the Louisiana Purchase and search for a water route to the Pacific Ocean.

1805 Nearly starving, the expedition reaches what is now Idaho, where members are aided by the Shoshone and the Nez Percé.

Traders and Travelers

1806 Lewis and Clark report back that the Idaho region has many fur-bearing animals. Soon after, fur traders begin to explore the area.

1830 Captain Benjamin Bonneville escorts the first wagon train across southern Idaho, and in 1834 Fort Hall and Fort Boise are established.

First Settlements

1836 Henry Harmon and Eliza Spalding found a mission among the Nez Percé. He becomes the first person to grow potatoes in Idaho. They build the first Idaho **gristmill**.

1860 Mormon families go to Idaho from Utah, and 13 families found Franklin, Idaho's first permanent white settlement.

Territory and Statehood

1860 Elias D. Pierce and a group of prospectors find a startling amount of gold at Orofino Creek in the Clearwater River region of northern Idaho. Mining towns spring up.

1863 U.S. President Abraham Lincoln establishes the Idaho Territory.

1890 Idaho becomes the 43rd state.

Early Settlers

During the 1840s and 1850s an estimated 53,000 people left homes farther east and passed through the Idaho region, but very few of them actually settled in the area. They were moving westward along the Oregon Trail to the fertile farmland of Oregon and, they hoped, to the rich gold fields of California.

Map of Settlements and Resources in Early Idaho

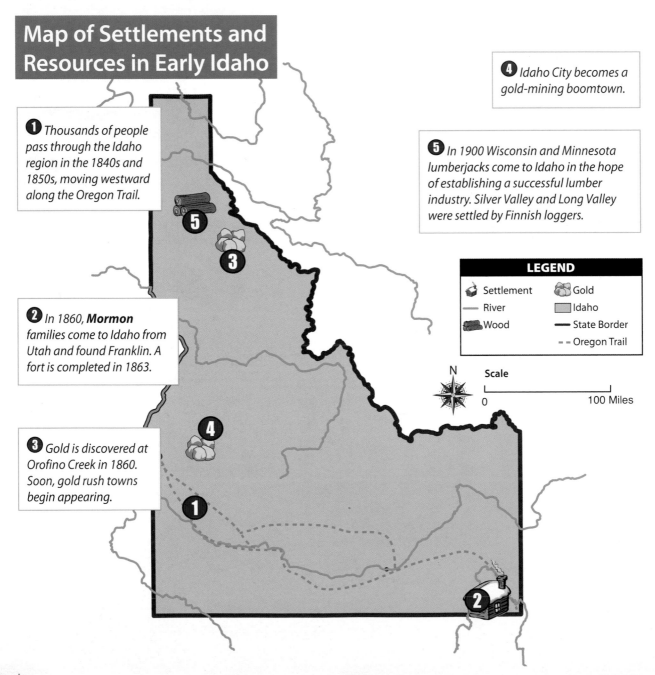

4 *Idaho City becomes a gold-mining boomtown.*

1 *Thousands of people pass through the Idaho region in the 1840s and 1850s, moving westward along the Oregon Trail.*

5 *In 1900 Wisconsin and Minnesota lumberjacks come to Idaho in the hope of establishing a successful lumber industry. Silver Valley and Long Valley were settled by Finnish loggers.*

2 *In 1860,* **Mormon** *families come to Idaho from Utah and found Franklin. A fort is completed in 1863.*

3 *Gold is discovered at Orofino Creek in 1860. Soon, gold rush towns begin appearing.*

LEGEND

🪣	Settlement	🍿	Gold
—	River	▨	Idaho
🪵	Wood	━	State Border
		- -	Oregon Trail

N

Scale

0   100 Miles

In April 1860 a number of Mormon families came to Idaho from Utah. The Mormons founded what was to become Idaho's first permanent settlement. They named their town Franklin, after a figure in their church. The new settlement was situated in the southeastern part of the state. The settlers worked hard to survive in their new home. They dug **irrigation** ditches and proved that the dry soil in the southern region could be used for farming. Soon after, other Mormon pioneers settled in the southern part of the state.

That same year, gold was found in northern Idaho, and prospectors began to pour into the state. Idaho's gold-mining days were often quite rowdy. Violence and thefts were commonplace in many of the towns. On March 4, 1863, U.S. President Abraham Lincoln created the Idaho Territory, in part so that the government could bring order to its mining towns.

Idaho's gold rush lasted only about 10 years, but it provided the basis for permanent settlement in the region. People from other parts of the United States learned that Idaho had fertile farmland, thick forests, and mineral resources.

At one of the main cutoffs on the Oregon Trail, travelers had to choose between heading toward Soda Springs, Idaho, or Sublette Cutoff, in Wyoming. The cutoff was shorter, but at Soda Springs, carbon dioxide bubbled up in the water, and many wanted to see it.

I DIDN'T KNOW THAT!

In 1846 Great Britain gave up its claim to the land in the Northwest south of the current Canada–United States border. As a result the Idaho region belonged officially to the United States. It was at first part of the vast Oregon Territory.

Many Chinese workers came to Idaho to work as miners during the gold rush.

During the gold rush, Idaho City had close to 40,000 residents. In the second half of the 1800s, it was one of the region's biggest mining settlements. It had lively saloons, theaters, and even an opera house.

New settlements led to fights between American Indians and the U.S. Army. The Nez Percé, one of the largest Indian groups, fought the Nez Percé War in 1877.

Electricity was turned on in Idaho in 1882 in the mining town of Hailey.

Notable People

Idaho has been a state only since 1890. However, the region that became Idaho is the birthplace or adopted home of numerous Americans whose lives have had historical significance. The people of Idaho have made important contributions in business, education, politics, sports, and other fields.

SACAGAWEA (c.1788–1812)

Sacagawea was a Shoshone woman born in the area that is now Idaho. As a young woman, she traveled with Lewis and Clark on their expedition and acted as an interpreter between the explorers and the different groups of American Indians that they encountered. She is one of the most popular figures in Idaho history.

GREGORY "PAPPY" BOYINGTON (1912–1988)

Gregory Boyington was an ace flyer for the Marine Corps in World War II. Assigned to the Solomon Islands in the Pacific, he commanded a squadron known as the "Black Sheep" and earned a reputation for shooting down enemy planes. The war hero himself was shot down and imprisoned for nearly two years. When the war ended, he was given the Medal of Honor.

CECIL ANDRUS (1931–)

When Cecil Andrus was re-elected as governor in 1974, it was by the widest margin in state history at that time. In 1977, he resigned as governor to serve as the U.S. secretary of the interior. In that post, he brought about the 1980 Alaska Lands Act, creating a number of national parks and wilderness areas in that state. He served as governor of Idaho again from 1987 to 1995.

LARRY ECHO HAWK (1948–)

A Pawnee Nation member and former Marine, Larry Echo Hawk began managing Indian trusts, land, and assets for the Department of the Interior in 2009. In 1990, he was elected attorney general of Idaho, the first American Indian in the post. From 1982 to 1986, he served in the Idaho House of Representatives.

BARBARA MORGAN (1951–)

Though born in California, Barbara Morgan was a teacher in Idaho when she was selected for NASA's "teacher in space" program. She was the backup for Christa McAuliffe, the teacher-astronaut who died when the *Challenger* exploded during its 1986 launch. Twenty-one years later, Morgan became the first teacher-astronaut in space.

I DIDN'T KNOW THAT!

Gutzon Borglum (1867–1941), the sculptor who made the Mt. Rushmore National Memorial, was born in St. Charles. He carved the faces of Presidents George Washington, Thomas Jefferson, Theodore Roosevelt, and Abraham Lincoln in a mountainside in the Black Hills of southwestern South Dakota.

Frank Church (1924 –1984), a U.S. senator from 1957 to 1981, served in the U.S. Army in World War II and worked as a lawyer before dedicating himself to public service in the U.S. Senate. He led efforts to preserve Idaho's wilderness areas.

Population

Most Idahoans live in the southern part of the state or in the western half of the panhandle. The mountainous areas of central and northern Idaho are nearly uninhabited. There are only a few remote communities in this wilderness. Idaho's rugged landscape has created a sense of **regionalism** within the state. Mountain ranges and desert areas are natural barriers that divide the state and isolate regions from one another.

Idaho Population 1950–2010

Idaho's population is almost three times as large as it was in 1950. What are some of the reasons for this growth?

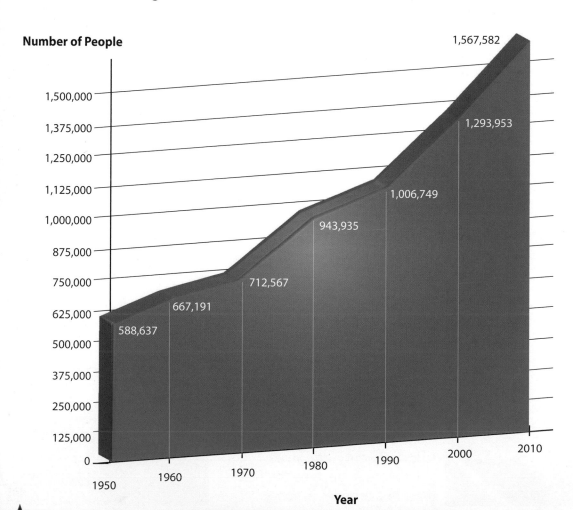

Number of People

- 1950: 588,637
- 1960: 667,191
- 1970: 712,567
- 1980: 943,935
- 1990: 1,006,749
- 2000: 1,293,953
- 2010: 1,567,582

Year

Transportation is difficult in the mountains. Many supplies must be flown to smaller communities by helicopters and small planes.

Most Idahoans live in the Snake River valley.

Boise, the state capital, is Idaho's largest city. The next largest city is Nampa.

The Idaho population is served by five state colleges, three state universities, and eleven private colleges and universities.

The center of population in Idaho is Custer County. The center of population is a geographic spot that is the center point around which the inhabitants live. It is used as the "average" location by people who keep track of population data.

In the 1990s the state's population increased by more than 28 percent. Yet in 2000 Idaho still had a **population density** of only 15.6 people per square mile. This was much lower than the national average of 80 people per square mile. In the 2010 Census, Idaho had a population of more than 1.5 million people but was still ranked 39th in the nation.

The majority of Idahoans live in the cities, such as Lewiston.

Politics and Government

In 1863, when the Idaho Territory was created, Lewiston, in the northern part of the territory, was chosen as the capital. Soon, though, the vast distances and high mountains between Lewiston and other communities made the government reconsider. In 1864 the capital was moved from Lewiston to Boise, which was larger and more accessible to the settlements in the south. People in northern Idaho were angry.

Boise is the state capital and also the county seat for Ada County.

Because of such regional differences, a plan to make northern Idaho part of Washington and southern Idaho part of Nevada was nearly put into effect in the mid-1880s. However, on July 3, 1890, Idaho became the 43rd state of the Union with Boise as the capital.

As in other states, Idaho's government has three branches. The legislative branch creates new laws and can change existing laws. The judicial branch interprets these laws, and the executive branch makes sure that the laws are carried out.

Idaho ranks among the top states in the amount of cropland under irrigation. Water rights are carefully regulated by the government.

The Idaho state song is called "Here We Have Idaho."

Here is an excerpt from the song:

You've heard of the wonders our land does possess, Its beautiful valleys and hills. The majestic forests where nature abounds, We love every nook and rill

Chorus:

And here we have Idaho, Winning her way to fame. Silver and gold in the sunlight blaze, And romance lies in her name. Singing, we're singing of you, Ah, proudly too. All our lives thru, We'll go singing, singing of you, Singing of Idaho.

Cultural Groups

Idaho is proud of its rich heritage and holds exhibitions and festivals that highlight the importance of the diverse ethnic groups living within the state. At the Idaho State Historical Museum, visitors can trace Idaho's history from the days of fur trading and mining camps to the development of Boise. The museum puts special emphasis on the contributions provided by various peoples, including the Basques, the Chinese, and the Shoshone.

The Basques are one of the most distinct ethnic groups in the state. During the 1800s people from the Basque region of northern Spain came to Idaho. Many were experienced shepherds and discovered that it was profitable to provide meat and wool to the area's miners. Today most Idahoans of Basque descent live in the Boise area. They celebrate their traditions at festivals and on religious holidays. During the Sheepherders' Ball, Basques wear colorful costumes and play lively folk music.

Basques no longer dominate the sheep industry as they once did, but the Basque community still celebrates this aspect of its history.

The gold rush of the 1860s brought many Chinese people to Idaho. When the gold rush ended, some Chinese stayed in the area to run businesses or to farm. Today descendants of these early Chinese settlers continue to make their homes in Idaho. Chinese cultural events and festivities, such as Chinese New Year, take place regularly.

American Indians in Idaho display great pride in their heritage. At the Fort Hall Reservation, near Pocatello, the Shoshone-Bannock Indian Festival celebrates traditional American Indian dress, dances, parades, and crafts. The Nez Percé of Lapwai hold traditional dancing celebrations during Chief Looking Glass Days in August. The Coeur d'Alene Indian Pilgrimage also takes place in August. This annual pilgrimage brings the Coeur d'Alene back to the Cataldo Mission, which was built by their ancestors more than 150 years ago. After a mass, a dinner is held, followed by traditional dancing, singing, and drumming.

Idaho's powwows include Julyamsh, advertised as the largest powwow in the Northwest.

I DIDN'T KNOW THAT!

The very popular Sheepherders' Ball takes place in Boise in December. The evening is celebrated with traditional Basque dancing and food. Ceremonial dancers carry wooden hoops, which they slap together in mock combat.

The Basque community has a large presence in Boise. Related organizations include numerous Basque dancing, singing, and musical groups. Basque restaurants, markets, and social and cultural centers can be found in the city.

The Shoshone-Bannock Indian Festival is held in August. It is hosted by the Fort Hall Reservation.

A Hispanic Heritage Fiesta is held annually at Twin Falls. The fiesta celebrates the heritage of Idaho's Hispanic Americans.

The Cataldo Mission is the oldest building in Idaho. It was built by missionaries and more than 300 Coeur d'Alene Indians.

Arts and Entertainment

I daho's early mining settlements had small theaters and opera houses where musical shows and plays were performed. Today Idaho continues to celebrate and enjoy music, theater, and art.

Musical concerts and festivals take place throughout the year. The Boise Philharmonic is the state's most prominent orchestra, but orchestras in Idaho Falls, Pocatello, and Moscow also entertain audiences. Many of Idaho's colleges and universities also have impressive symphonies. In fact, numerous state schools have strong music departments, where students can develop their musical talents. The Lionel Hampton School of Music at the University of Idaho is a well-respected learning center. Named after the famous jazz bandleader, it hosts the Lionel Hampton Jazz Festival each year. The Lionel Hampton Center also has a significant archive of jazz information and memorabilia.

Idaho celebrates cowboy culture as part of the state's heritage. Idaho rodeos, featuring steer wrestlers and skilled horse riders, are held throughout the spring, summer, and fall.

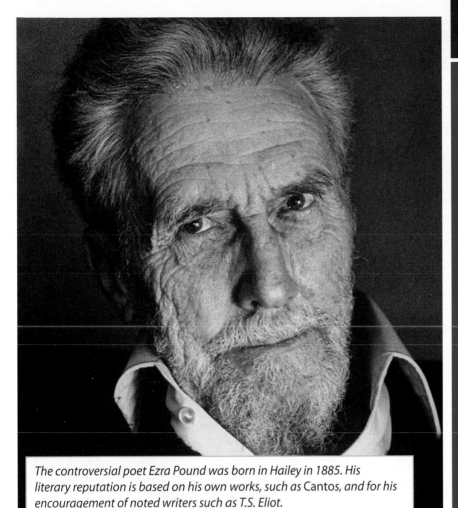

The controversial poet Ezra Pound was born in Hailey in 1885. His literary reputation is based on his own works, such as Cantos, and for his encouragement of noted writers such as T.S. Eliot.

There is more to Idaho's music scene than the classical sounds of its orchestras or the cool beats of its jazz festivals, however. At the National Old Time Fiddlers' Contest and Festival, audiences are treated to the lively tunes of some of the world's finest fiddlers. The event, held annually in Weiser, is one of the state's many folk music festivals.

Idaho delights in visual arts, too. The Boise Art Museum, known as BAM, houses a collection of local, national, and international artwork. In addition to its permanent exhibits, the museum hosts an event called Art in the Park. This outdoor exhibition takes place in Boise's Julia Davis Park and features the work of hundreds of artists

Jon Heder played the title character in *Napoleon Dynamite*, filmed in Preston, in Franklin County. The town of Preston has become a tourist attraction.

The Idaho Shakespeare Festival takes place during the summer at an outdoor **amphitheater** in Boise.

Ernest Hemingway worked on his novel *For Whom the Bell Tolls* while visiting Idaho. He later returned, spending his last years in Ketchum before his death in 1961.

At Idaho's rodeos, even kids get in on the act. The "mutton busting" events feature children on sheep.

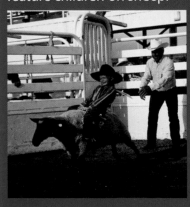

Sports

Idaho is a great place for outdoor enthusiasts, nature lovers, and thrill seekers. Throughout the spring and summer months, hikers and backpackers can trek along Idaho's mountain trails and camp in the state's many campgrounds. Swimmers can go for a dip in one of the beautiful lakes in northern Idaho or further south in the lakes of the Sawtooth National Recreation Area. Idaho's lakes are also used for sailing, fishing, or canoeing.

More adventurous water lovers can raft, canoe, or kayak on one of the state's quick-flowing rivers. Licensed outfitters offer guided rafting trips down rushing waterways. Experienced kayakers come to the state to ride the white-water rapids of the Selway, Salmon, or Snake rivers.

During the winter, Idaho has some of the best skiing in North America. Among the state's most popular ski resorts are Sun Valley, Silver Mountain, Schweitzer Mountain, and Bogus Basin. The resorts cater to beginners and advanced skiers alike. Olympians such as Picabo Street, Christin Cooper, Bill Johnson, and Gretchen Fraser all have trained on Idaho's slopes.

The Sun Valley Resort is a popular year-round travel destination. Summertime activities include horseback riding, swimming, biking, and hiking.

Snowboarders can practice their form in the Bitterroot, Grand Teton, and Sawtooth mountain ranges.

Sun Valley, which opened in 1936, is the state's most famous ski resort. It offers its visitors excellent downhill and cross-country ski trails. It also has trails for snowshoeing and snowmobiling as well as places for ice skating. In fact, the resort boasts a world-class ice-skating rink.

The Winter Games of Idaho, held in Boise, cater to outdoor enthusiasts with a competitive edge. This sports festival gathers thousands of amateur athletes in such events as freestyle skiing, snowboarding, ice hockey, figure skating, snowmobiling, and Alpine and cross-country ski racing.

I DIDN'T KNOW THAT!

The talented football star Jerry Kramer attended the University of Idaho. He played for the Green Bay Packers from 1958 to 1968 as an offensive lineman and kicker.

Picabo Street, from Triumph, is a world-champion downhill skier. She won a gold medal at the 1998 Winter Olympics in Nagano, Japan, and a silver medal at the 1994 Olympics in Lillehammer, Norway. She began skiing at the age of 6 at Sun Valley.

A Ketchum resident named Dick Fosbury invented the popular high-jump technique known as the Fosbury Flop.

Harmon Killebrew, a talented baseball player from Payette, signed with the Washington Senators when he was only 17 years old. Killebrew, a powerful home-run hitter, was inducted into the Baseball Hall of Fame in 1984.

Reggie and Zach Crist were raised in Sun Valley. The two brothers exhibit legendary form on the ski slopes. They are the first sibling pair to both have won X Games titles.

National Averages Comparison

The United States is a federal republic, consisting of fifty states and the District of Columbia. Alaska and Hawai'i are the only non-contiguous, or non-touching, states in the nation. Today, the United States of America is the third-largest country in the world in population. The United States Census Bureau takes a census, or count of all the people, every ten years. It also regularly collects other kinds of data about the population and the economy. How does Idaho compare to the national average?

Comparison Chart

United States 2010 Census Data *	USA	Idaho
Admission to Union	NA	July 3, 1890
Land Area (in square miles)	3,537,438.44	82,747.21
Population Total	308,745,538	1,567,582
Population Density (people per square mile)	87.28	18.94
Population Percentage Change (April 1, 2000, to April 1, 2010)	9.7%	21.1%
White Persons (percent)	72.4%	89.1%
Black Persons (percent)	12.6%	0.6%
American Indian and Alaska Native Persons (percent)	0.9%	1.4%
Asian Persons (percent)	4.8%	1.2%
Native Hawaiian and Other Pacific Islander Persons (percent)	0.2%	0.1%
Some Other Race (percent)	6.2%	5.1%
Persons Reporting Two or More Races (percent)	2.9%	2.5%
Persons of Hispanic or Latino Origin (percent)	16.3%	11.2%
Not of Hispanic or Latino Origin (percent)	83.7%	88.8%
Median Household Income	$52,029	$47,561
Percentage of People Age 25 or Over Who Have Graduated from High School	80.4%	84.7%

*All figures are based on the 2010 United States Census, with the exception of the last two items.

How to Improve My Community

Strong communities make strong states. Think about what features are important in your community. What do you value? Education? Health? Forests? Safety? Beautiful spaces? Government works to help citizens create ideal living conditions that are fair to all by providing services in communities. Consider what changes you could make in your community. How would they improve your state as a whole? Using this concept web as a guide, write a report that outlines the features you think are most important in your community and what improvements could be made. A strong state needs strong communities.

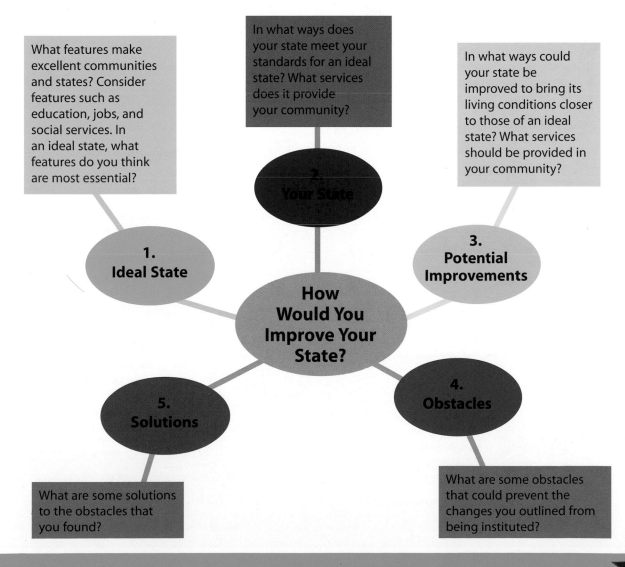

What features make excellent communities and states? Consider features such as education, jobs, and social services. In an ideal state, what features do you think are most essential?

In what ways does your state meet your standards for an ideal state? What services does it provide your community?

In what ways could your state be improved to bring its living conditions closer to those of an ideal state? What services should be provided in your community?

2. Your State

1. Ideal State

3. Potential Improvements

How Would You Improve Your State?

4. Obstacles

5. Solutions

What are some solutions to the obstacles that you found?

What are some obstacles that could prevent the changes you outlined from being instituted?

Exercise Your Mind!

Think about these questions and then use your research skills to find the answers and learn more fascinating facts about Idaho. A teacher, librarian, or parent may be able to help you locate the best sources to use in your research.

1 True or False? Sacagawea carried a baby with her on the Lewis and Clark Expedition.

2 True or False? Astronauts who took part in early moon missions trained at Craters of the Moon.

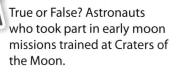

3 Which of the following is not a town in Idaho?

A. Moscow
B. Atlanta
C. Paris
D. Milan

4 True or False? On Oct. 28, 1983, Borah Peak grew one foot higher.

5 Which of the following technological advances has roots in Rigby?

A. microwave
B. television
C. cellular phone
D. wheel

6 True or False? The world's first Alpine skiing chairlift is located in Sun Valley.

7 Which major Idaho city was named for its many trees?

8 Julia Jean Mildred Frances Turner, born in Wallace, became one of Hollywood's favorite stars of the 1940s and 1950s. What was her stage name?

Words to Know

amphitheater: round or oval building with a semicircular seating arrangement

archaeologists: scientists who study ancient cultures by examining their ruins and remains

barge: a flat-bottomed boat that carries large shipments of goods, usually on canals or rivers

capitol: building for the legislature

expedition: a journey made for exploration

gorge: a steep and narrow valley

gristmill: a mill that grinds grain

hydroelectric power: electricity created using the force of moving water

irrigation: supplying water to dry regions

locks: chambers in a canal or dam that lower or raise the water level so that ships may pass through

Mormon: belonging to the Church of Jesus Christ of Latter-Day Saints

petroglyphs: ancient carvings on rock

phenomenon: a fact or event, often rare or sigificant

pictographs: ancient paintings or drawings on rock

population density: the average number of people per unit of area

precious: of great value

prospector: person who searches for valuable mineral deposits

regionalism: pride in one's own region

transcontinental: crossing or stretching across a continent

Index

American Indians 26, 27, 29, 31, 32, 39
Andrus, Cecil 33

Balanced Rock 21
Basques 38, 39
Bitterroot Mountains 10, 21, 28
Boise 9, 13, 15, 21, 23, 25, 35, 36, 37, 38, 39, 40, 41, 43
Borah Peak 7, 46
Borglum, Gutzon 33
Boyington, Gregory 32

Cataldo Mission 39
Church, Frank 33
Clark, William 21, 28, 29

Coeur d'Alene 17, 27, 39
Columbia River 25
Craters of the Moon National Monument and Preserve 17, 20, 46

Echo Hawk, Larry 33

Hells Canyon 11, 24, 26

Idaho City 13, 30, 31

Ketchum 41, 43

Lewis, Meriwether 21, 28, 29
Lewiston 23, 24, 28, 35, 36

mining 5, 6, 7, 15, 29
Minnetonka Cave 21

Old Idaho Penitentiary 21
Oregon Trail 28, 30, 31

panhandle 17

Sacagawea 32
Salmon River 4, 6, 26, 42
Snake River 4, 10, 11, 14, 15, 20, 26, 42
Spalding, Eliza 28, 29
Spalding, Henry 28, 29
Sun Valley 20, 42, 43, 46

Log on to www.av2books.com

AV² by Weigl brings you media enhanced books that support active learning. Go to www.av2books.com, and enter the special code found on page 2 of this book. You will gain access to enriched and enhanced content that supplements and complements this book. Content includes video, audio, web links, quizzes, a slide show, and activities.

Audio
Listen to sections of the book read aloud.

Video
Watch informative video clips.

Embedded Weblinks
Gain additional information for research.

Try This!
Complete activities and hands-on experiments.

WHAT'S ONLINE?

Try This!	Embedded Weblinks	Video	EXTRA FEATURES
Test your knowledge of the state in a mapping activity.	Discover more attractions in Idaho.	Watch a video introduction to Idaho.	**Audio** Listen to sections of the book read aloud.
Find out more about precipitation in your city.	Learn more about the history of the state.	Watch a video about the features of the state.	
Plan what attractions you would like to visit in the state.	Learn the full lyrics of the state song.		**Key Words** Study vocabulary, and complete a matching word activity.
Learn more about the early natural resources of the state.			
Write a biography about a notable resident of Idaho.			**Slide Show** View images and captions, and prepare a presentation.
Complete an educational census activity.			**Quizzes** Test your knowledge.

AV² was built to bridge the gap between print and digital. We encourage you to tell us what you like and what you want to see in the future.

Sign up to be an AV² Ambassador at www.av2books.com/ambassador.